Disney · PIXAR
THE GOOD DINOSAUR
STICKER SCENES

PaRragon

Bath · New York · Cologne · Melbourne · Delhi
Hong Kong · Shenzhen · Singapore · Amsterdam

Meet the dinosaurs

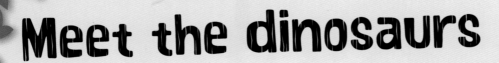

In a world where dinosaurs never became extinct, two Apatosauruses live on a farm with their three children — Buck, Libby and Arlo.

Arlo is the youngest. He is happy, but he is also frightened of everything! Most of all, Arlo is scared of the wilderness that lies beyond the fence at the edge of the farm.

One night, Poppa takes Arlo into one of the fields on the farm. Suddenly, an insect lands on Arlo's nose. Arlo is scared, but Henry tells his son to stand still and then blows gently on the insect — and it glows!

Next, Henry sweeps his tail through the grass and hundreds of fireflies fly into the sky. They are beautiful!

The little dinosaur looks at his Poppa and smiles.

The critter hunt

One day, a critter steals some corn from the farm. The critter is a little human boy. Henry decides to teach Arlo to be brave, so he takes his son on a critter hunt!

Father and son head into the wilderness, but they get lost in a storm and poor Henry is swept away in a flood! Arlo is heartbroken. He will never see his Poppa again.

Back at the farm, life is hard without Henry. Arlo's Momma is very tired from the extra work she has to do. Arlo tries his best to help her and take care of his family.

One day, as Arlo is working hard, he sees the same critter stealing more corn! Arlo and the critter wrestle, and they tumble backwards into the river.

"Momma, Momma, Momma!" Arlo cries, but he has already been swept too far away for anyone to hear.

Arlo struggles to keep afloat as the river carries him away. Then suddenly — *BAM!* The little dinosaur hits his head on a rock and he is pulled under by the current.

Lost in the wilderness

When Arlo wakes up, he realizes he is lost. His head and legs hurt, and he is all alone. Before long, he feels raindrops on his head and decides to build a shelter using twigs and branches.

Little forest creatures peek out of their homes to watch Arlo at work. Arlo feels like they must be laughing at him. He has never built anything in his life!

Once his shelter is complete, Arlo curls up beneath its leaky roof. But, seconds later, he hears something rustling in the bushes outside, heading in his direction....

Title page

Meet the dinosaurs

Just for fun

© Disney/Pixar

© Disney/Pixar

© Disney/Pixar

Just for fun

Braver than ever

Just for fun

Surviving the storm

Just for fun

Home at last

The critter hunt

Lost in
the wilderness

Arlo peers nervously out of his shelter and sees ... the critter!

"Get outta here!" shouts Arlo. But the boy won't go. He brings Arlo some berries to eat. The dinosaur and the boy become friends.

Arlo gives the boy a name — Spot. Together, they try to find a way back to Arlo's farm. Spot can't talk, but he and Arlo find a way of communicating by making figures out of twigs — and howling!

Arlo learns that Spot has lost his family, just as Arlo has lost his Poppa. The new friends are glad that they have found each other.

A few days later, Arlo and Spot meet a T. rex called Butch and his
family, who have lost their herd of longhorns. Arlo offers to help the
T. rexes search for the longhorns, if the T. rexes can show him the
direction home. Butch agrees, and the group use Spot's incredible
sense of smell to track down the herd. But a nasty surprise awaits....

Raptors! This gang of crooks has stolen the longhorns.

"Hold your ground!" Butch says to Arlo as the Raptors attack.

Arlo is brave, even though the rustlers are much stronger than he is.
Eventually, the Raptors give up and run away.

"You're one tough kid," Butch says to Arlo. The T. rexes are pleased to have their longhorns back.

Arlo and Spot continue on their journey, heading into the misty mountains. As they wander together taking in the beautiful scenery, Arlo spots Clawtooth Mountain in the distance. He can find his way home, at last!

Surviving the storm

Arlo and Spot continue along the mountain path. After a while, Spot points up at the sky. There is something wrong.

Arlo looks up and sees some Pterodactyls swooping down towards them! The flying hunters catch hold of Spot and whisk him up and away into the gathering storm clouds.

"Spot!" screams Arlo as he watches his friend disappear. "No!"

Arlo gives chase, howling into the storm. Arlo sees the boy and feels a surge of courage in his heart. He charges at the Pterodactyls and drives them away.

Spot is so pleased to see his friend again, but there is no time to celebrate. A storm is raging and the river is filling up fast.

Suddenly, a wall of water sweeps Arlo and Spot away! Then Arlo sees something scary — a waterfall, straight ahead!

Arlo grabs hold of Spot as they tumble over the waterfall and fall into the river far below. They land with a mighty *SPLASH!*

After a moment, Arlo bobs to the surface, holding Spot. They have survived! They climb on to the river bank, feeling so happy to be alive.

Home at Last

Arlo and Spot set off once again. Soon, they are both amazed to see a human family emerge from the forest! Arlo knows that Spot will be happier with his own people, so he pushes him towards the family. The two friends sadly say goodbye.

Arlo continues alone. But, before long, he sees something that makes him very happy — his family's farm. He's home!